THE
AUGUST
BABY

THE
August
BABY

Noel Streatfeild

First published in 1959
This edition published in 2023 by Headline Home
an imprint of Headline Publishing Group

1

Cataloguing in Publication Data is available from the British Library

Hardback ISBN 978 1 0354 0853 5
eISBN 978 1 0354 0854 2

Typeset in 14.75/15pt Centaur MT Pro by Jouve (UK), Milton Keynes

Printed and bound in Great Britain by Clays Ltd, Elcograf S.p.A.

HEADLINE PUBLISHING GROUP
An Hachette UK Company
Carmelite House
50 Victoria Embankment
London EC4Y 0DZ

www.headline.co.uk
www.hachette.co.uk

CONTENTS

AUGUST is the care-free away-from-it-all month, made this year the more care-free because your baby has been born. What a to-and-fro-ing of messages from holiday-makers both at home and abroad there has been. Your room, most probably, is at this moment decorated with congratulatory postcards from faraway places, all saying the sender cannot wait to get home to see you and the August baby.

Delighted though everybody is that you have an August baby, so convenient to have a birthday which will always be celebrated during the holidays, August is a tiresome month for gifts. No month in the year is more difficult for flowers. There are of course the usual standbys, such as carnations, but of flowers belonging to the month there are very few. The most beautiful are perhaps the gladiolus, but gladioli are a great strain on

reserves of vases, for only the high vase suits them. So too many gladioli can cause sighs from the nurse.

Fruit is equally difficult, unless your baby was born in the north, for in most of the country the strawberries and the raspberries are over, and unless it is a particularly hot summer such delicacies as figs are not ripe, so the visitor thinks twice about a present of fruit.

A present of something for the mother to wear is always acceptable, but there again August is a betwixt and between month, too early for the quilted or knitted bed-jacket, and rather late for something diaphanous made of nylon and lace. A present for the baby is perfect, but so few of us are strong-minded enough to hold back the pull-ups and the pram coat until the baby is actually there. It is so much easier to send the present in advance, when both blue and pink are perfectly correct.

The present most women want to bring is a toy for the baby, and August is a tempting month for that sort of shopping. The toy shop is full of parents buying buckets and spades and shrimping nets, but that part reserved for soft toys is left undisturbed. It is then that friends and relations can wallow

amongst delicious animals, that little soft lion cub, that pale blue monkey that can hang on to anything by its tail, that small poodle divinely clipped with the plus-fours and topknot of real wool. But does baby want a monkey that can hang on by its tail, a woolly poodle, or a lion cub? And do you? Very nice perhaps while you are actually in bed, but apt to collect dust and even moths before baby can appreciate a toy.

It is years of wondering what to bring

mother and child that has resulted in this book. What do you talk about when you've finished admiring the baby, and asked after the mother's health? Baby of course, nothing but baby, so here then is a book, not weighty, but full of information about past and present August children.

It is an odd thing but there are countless parents who wait for the baby to be born before they come to a decision about a name.

Sometimes a name has been chosen, but it sounds awful with the surname, so a second is wanted, and quite often no name has been chosen at all, even when the christening has been arranged. So here, for the parents' perusal, is a list of names all more or less connected with August.

You may not believe those columns in the papers that tell you what the stars foretell, but few of us can resist information about the sign under which we were born. But in this book, as well as information about the zodiac signs, there is also a list for your perusal of famous people born on each day in August, and very surprising you will probably find it. Admitting that both were typical Leo babies, would you expect to find Isaak Walton and Leonide Massine sharing a birthday? Or if it comes to that, who would guess that Albert the Prince Consort and John Buchan were born on the same day?

At one time mothers in bed after the birth of their child had what many wistfully describe as the only peaceful times they ever knew, for a whole month in bed it was. Now, far from being a month the time spent in bed gets shorter and shorter, and far from being restful you are doing exercises before you know what your baby looks like. But you may perhaps snatch a minute here and there for light reading, and it was for that possibility this offering was compiled.

NAMES
for the
AUGUST
BABY

AUGUST was named by the Romans after Augustus Cæsar. *Augustus* means 'venerable', and so do *Augustine, Austin* and *Sebastian*, and *Augusta* for a girl.

August was not the month in which Augustus Cæsar was born, but that of his triumphs. Here are some names to do with triumph and victory. *Victor* and *Victoria* for a girl, mean 'conqueror', and *Vincent* 'conquering'. A laurel wreath was a symbol of victory, *Laurence* and *Lawrence* mean 'laurel', and for girls *Laura, Lauren* or *Lauretta*. One of the triumphs of Augustus Cæsar belongs to

August, for it was in this month he put an end to the civil war then raging in Rome, which makes you think of the name *Geoffrey* or *Jeffrey* which means 'district-peace'. Other

names which have the same sort of meanings are *Freda, Frida, Frieda* and *Irene* which all mean 'peace'. *Manfred* is 'man of peace'. A symbol of peace is the dove, carrying an olive branch in its beak. *Colan, Colin* and *Colman* mean 'dove', Columba is the latin word for 'dove', and the name *Malcolm* means 'disciple of Columba': *Columbine* means 'dove-like', and *Jemima* 'dove'.

Three names meaning 'olive' are *Oliver, Olive* and *Olivia.*

The special apostle assigned to August is St James son of Alpheus. *James* means 'supplanter'.

The sign of the zodiac for part of August is Virgo the Virgin. *Virginia* means 'virgin', and names connected with virgins are *Catherine, Cathleen, Catlin, Karen, Kate, Katharine, Katrine, Kay, Agnes, Annot, Ines, Inez* and *Nesta,* all of which mean 'pure'.

'White' is associated with purity, and these all mean 'white': *Albina, Bianca, Blanche, Candida, Gwen, Gwenda, Gwynne* and *Winne.* 'White' is also part of many girls' names, for instance *Blodwen* means 'white flower', *Bronwen* 'white breast', *Fenella*, *Finella* and *Finola* mean 'white shoulder', *Gwendolyn* 'white-browed', *Meriel* and *Muriel* 'sea-white', *Olwen* 'white track', and *Rowena* 'white skirt'. *Gaynor*, *Guinevere* (shades of King Arthur), *Jennifer*, *Vanora* and *Winifred* all mean 'white wave'.

The first of August is today called Lammas day, but from earliest times it was the great harvest festival of pagan Britain. Here are some names to do with harvest and the land. *Teresa* or *Theresa* mean 'reaper', *George* 'farmer', or for girls *Georgia*, *Georgiana* and *Georgina*. *Payne* means 'countryman'. Many names originally were place-names which would not mean much to people today, so here is a list without meanings, of some names of territorial origin. For girls, *Doris*, *Loretta*, *Lucasta*, *Lydia*, *Madeleine*, *Madeline*, *Magda*, *Magdalen*, *Mercia*, *Shirley* and *Sidney*. For boys there is also a long list: *Bruce*, *Carlisle*, *Carlyle*, *Chauncey*, *Ciprian*, *Cyprian*, *Clifford*, *Courtenay*, *Darcy*, *Desmond*, *Dudley*, *Gordon*, *Graham*, *Hallam*, *Keith*, *Leslie*, *Lester*, *Granville*, *Lucas*, *Luke*, *Percy*, *Sidney* or *Sydney*, *Vere* and *Winston*.

The 4th of August is St Dominic's Day. *Dominic* or *Dominick* means 'of the Lord'.

The 5th of August is St Thomas of Dover's Day. *Thomas* means 'twin'.

The 9th of August is St Oswald's Day. *Oswald* means 'divine power' and so does

Oswell. Here are some other names containing the old English prefix 'os'. *Osbert* 'divinely bright', *Osborn* 'divine man', *Oscar* 'divine spear'. *Osmond* 'divine protection', *Osred* 'divine counsel', and *Osric* 'divine rule'.

Back to the Roman calendar to August the 13th which is the day on which the festival of Diana goddess of chastity was kept. *Diana* also is associated with hunting.

St Oswin's Day is on the 20th of August. *Oswin* means 'divine friend'.

St Bernard's Day is also on the 20th August. *Bernard* means 'brave as a bear'.

St Eugene's Day is the 23rd of August. *Eugene* and *Eugenie* mean 'well-born'.

St Owen shares the 24th with St Bartholomew the Apostle. *Owen* also means 'well-born', and *Bartholomew* means 'abounding in furrows'.

The 25th is the day of St Gregory of Utrecht. *Gregory* means 'to be watchful'.

St Adrian's Day is the 26th of August. *Adrian* means 'black'.

The 27th of August is the Blessed Amyas' Day. *Amyas* means 'a man beloved' and is alas seldom used nowadays.

The 29th of August is the Blessed Richard Herst's Day. *Richard* means 'stern ruler.'

And last of all for this month is St Aidan's Day on the 31st of August. *Aidan* means 'fire'.

The stone for all August is the Peridot. *Peridot,* though never used, could be a charming Christian name for either a boy or a girl.

GIFTS
for the
AUGUST
BABY

IF a godparent or any well-wisher would like to give a piece of jewellery to the August baby, the right gift is the peridot, that clear bright decorative lime-green stone; but they will probably sigh with relief that their godchildren have chosen so inexpensive a birthstone. It has a supposed valuable quality associated with it, for it is said to be a protection against insanity, but it must be admitted countless August babies who could not be more sane have never seen a peridot. Here is what Leonardus says in *The Mirror of Stones* about the peridot:

'. . . bound round with Gold, and carried in the left Hand, drives away Night-hags, and disperses Fears and melancholy Illusions. It is particularly efficacious in rendering ineffectual the Inclinations and Enchantments of those detestable Creatures call'd Witches. It being bor'd thro', and the Hairs of an Ass pass'd thro' it, its Virtue is the greater in driving away evil Spirits.'

The old custom of arranging flowers so that they bring a message, should be revived for an August baby. So if your child should receive a nosegay of ferns, balsam, snapdragons, sage and bitter-sweet nightshade, it will mean:

If by magic (ferns) such things could be given in a bouquet, one might give the August baby impatience (balsam), with presumption (snapdragons), and esteem (sage) for truth (bitter-sweet nightshade).

If your baby was born between the 1st and the 23rd of August read pages 24 and 25, but if between the 24th and the 31st of August, skip to pages 26 and 27.

20

UNDER
WHAT STARS WAS
MY BABY
BORN?

LEO
The Lion

24th July–23rd August

VIRGO
The Virgin

24th August–23rd September

LIBRA
The Scales

24th September–23rd October

SCORPIO
The Scorpion

24th October–22nd November

SAGITTARIUS
The Archer

23rd November–21st December

CAPRICORN
The Sea Goat

22nd December–20th January

AQUARIUS
The Water Bearer

21st January–19th February

PISCES
The Fishes

20th February–20th March

ARIES
The Ram

21st March–20th April

TAURUS
The Bull

21st April–21st May

GEMINI
The Twins

22nd May–21st June

CANCER
The Crab

22nd June–23rd July

Leo – the Lion
24th July–23rd August

TO be born under Leo is to be great-hearted: courageous and compassionate. Leo people are endowed with great stability and power, and their capacity for unswerving action is lessened never by any lack of determination in them but only by impulses of feeling for others. Their power in the world is enormous and of the permanent sort, for they never wield it ruthlessly. They often live in an ideal world of justice and harmony and do possess the organising ability needed to realise such a world, but wherever there is a choice between what is just and what is generous, feeling will outweigh judgment. Leo, with its emphasis on heart, is considered the best sign of the zodiac under which to be born.

For the Leo Baby

Lucky to wear diamond, jacynth.
Lucky stones are the sparkling ones, like quartz.
Lucky metal is gold.
The Leo baby's colour is orange.
Lucky numbers are 1 and 4.
Luckiest day is Sunday.

Virgo — the Virgin
24th August—23rd September

THE chief characteristic of Virgo persons is inward purity. They are going very much against the grain when they do not match this purity of mind with chastity. Whatever their lives externally, they do not cease to be of spiritual imagination. Equally endowed with intuition and with practical reasoning power and ingenuity, they are among the cleverest of the twelve types. They are studious, and conscientious to a worrisome degree. Virgo people are quite likely to have wit, but unlikely to have a sense of humour. A certain quality of detachment makes them slow to form friendships and not sure to maintain them. They have a tremendous capacity for devotion, but such a tendency to idealise and demand perfection of the people they love as to make for a stormy emotional life.

For the Virgo Baby

Lucky to wear topaz, amber.
Lucky stones are marble, glass.
Lucky metal is quicksilver.
The Virgo baby's colour is yellow.
Lucky number is 5.
Luckiest day is Wednesday.

BABIES BORN
ON
THE SAME DAY
AS
YOUR BABY

SHOULD you feel pleased that your baby was born on a particular day? Is there any truth in what the astrologers say about some birth days having special advantages, that babies born under Leo are like this, whereas babies born under Virgo are like that? Have a look at the well-known people in this list before you decide.

1st   Cavour, 1810. Herman Melville, 1819.

2nd   The Marquis of Granby, 1721. Cardinal Wiseman, 1802. John Tyndall, 1820. Sir Arthur Bliss, 1891.

3rd   Earl Baldwin, 1867. Haakon VII of Norway, 1872. Rupert Brooke, 1887. Leslie Henson, 1891. Dolores del Rio, 1905.

4th   Pope Urban VII, 1521. Edward Irving, 1792. Shelley, 1792. Walter Pater, 1839.

W. H. Hudson, 1841. The Queen Mother, 1900.

5th   Edmund of Woodstock, The Earl of Kent, 1301. Maupassant, 1850. Henri Groues, called 'Abbé Pierre,' 1910. Robert Taylor, 1911.

6th   Matthew Parker, Archbishop of Canterbury, 1504. Fénelon, 1651. Sir William Wallaston, 1766. Dora Wordsworth, 1804. Tennyson, 1809. Sir Alexander Fleming, 1881. John Middleton Murry, 1889. Field Marshal Sir William Slim, 1891. Sir Alvary Gascoigne, 1893. Robert Mitchum, 1917.

7th   Princess Amelia, 1783. Sir Granville Bantock, 1868.

8th   Lord Evershed, 1899. Robert H. Turton, 1903. Rory Calhoun, 1922.

9th   Izaak Walton, 1593. John Dryden, 1631. Léonide Massine, 1896. Armand Salacrou, 1899. Leo Genn, 1905.

10th   Sir Charles Napier, 1782. William Morrison, 1893.

11th   Charlotte M. Yonge, 1823. Thomas Betterton, 1635. Joseph Nollekens, 1737.

12th   George IV, 1762. Robert Southey, 1774. Cecil B. de Mille, 1881. Frank Swinnerton, 1884. Professor Joad, 1891.

13th   Théroigne de Méricourt, 1762. Alfred Hitchcock, 1899. Mrs Robert Henrey, 1906. Archbishop Makarios III, 1913.

14th   Paolo Sarpi, 1552. Dr Meric Casaubon, 1599. Pope Pius VII, 1740. Marie-Allard, 1742. John Galsworthy, 1867. Sir Harry Lauder, 1870.

15th   Ferdinand Columbus, 1488. Admiral Robert Blake, 1599. Jeremy Taylor, 1613. Frederick William I of Prussia, 1688. Napoleon, 1769. Sir Walter Scott, 1771. Thomas de Quincey, 1785. Keir Hardie, 1856. Francis Yeats-Brown, 1856. E. Nesbit, 1858. Baron Wrangel, 1878. Ethel Barrymore, 1879. T. E. Lawrence, 1888. John Cranko, 1927. Princess Anne, 1950.

16th   Catherine Cockburn, 1679. Antoine Lavoisier, 1743. Frederick, Duke of York, 1763. Ann Blyth, 1928.

17th   Thomas Stothard, 1755. Davy Crockett, 1786. Sir William Edward Rootes, 1894. Dame Caroline Haslett, 1895.

John Hay Whitney, 1904. Roy Tattersall, 1922.

18th   John, Earl Russell, 1792. Emperor Franz Joseph, 1830. Basil Cameron, 1884. Vijaya Lakshmi Pandit, 1900. Moura Lympany, 1916.

19th   The Admirable Crichton, 1560. Elizabeth Stuart, Queen of Bohemia, 1596. John Flamsteed, 1646. Dauberval, 1742. Jean Pierre de Béranger, 1780. Agnes Strickland, 1796. James Nasmyth, 1808. Bernard Baruch, 1870. Orville Wright, 1871. Rose Heilbron, 1914.

20th   Robert Herrick, 1591. Raymond Poincaré, 1860.

21st   Philip II of France, 1165. William IV, 1765. Claude Grahame-White, 1879. Princess Margaret, 1930.

22nd   Sir Tatton Sykes, 1772. Sir Alexander Campbell Mackenzie, 1847. Debussy, 1862. Lord Citrine, 1887.

23rd   Louis XVI of France, 1754. W. E. Henley, 1849. Geoffrey Faber, 1889. William Primrose, 1904.

24th   Alexander II of Scotland, 1198. Letizia Ramolini Bonaparte, 1750. William

Wilberforce, 1759. General Philippe Pétain, 1856. Sir Max Beerbohm, 1872.

25th   Herder, 1744. Bret Harte, 1836. Sean T. O'Kelly, 1882. Mel Ferrer, 1917.

26th   Sir Robert Walpole, 1st Earl of Orford, 1676. Albert The Prince Consort, 1819. John Buchan (Lord Tweedsmuir), 1875. The Sultan of Zanzibar, 1879. Apollinaire, 1880. Jules Romains, 1885. Christopher Isherwood, 1904. Prince Richard, 1944.

27th   Hegel, 1770. Louisa Fanny Pyne, 1832. Eric Coates, 1886. The Marquess of Salisbury, 1893. C. S. Forester, 1899. Sir Donald Bradman, 1908.

28th   George Villiers, 1st Duke of Buckingham, 1592. Johann Wolfgang von Goethe, 1749. Edward Burne-Jones, 1833. Charles Boyer, 1899. Van Johnson, 1916.

29th   John Locke, 1632. Ingres, 1780. Oliver Wendell Holmes, 1809. Maurice Maeterlinck, 1862. Ingrid Bergman, 1911. Richard Attenborough, 1923.

30th   Mary Wollstonecraft Shelley, 1797. J. M. Dent, 1849. Lord Rutherford

1871. Raymond Massey, 1896. Fred
MacMurray, 1908.

31st   Caius Caesar Caligula, A.D. 12. Théophile
Gautier, 1811. Princess Wilhelmina of
the Netherlands, 1880. The Earl of
Shaftesbury, 1869. Frederic March, 1897.

THE UPBRINGING OF AUGUST BABIES OF THE PAST

W HAT manner of Creature, a Nurse ought to be.

For her Person. She is of a middle stature, fleshy, but not fat; of a merry, pleasant cheerful countenance, a ruddy Colour, very cleer Skin that you may see her Veins through it.

For her Conditions. She loves Company, and cannot endure to be alone; not given to anger, but infinitly to playing and singing; she delights much in Children, and therefore is the fittest Nurse for one.

Culpeper, *A Directory for Midwives,* 1651.

Tears, by dissipating the superfluous Moisture of the Brain, and Crying, forasmuch as it opens and dilates the Lungs, provided they don't go too far, do Good to a young Child: But excessive Tears dry the Brain, and prevent sleeping; and obstinate and outrageous Crying, may burst the *Peritonæum,* and cause a *Hernia,* or Rupture. A Child weeps or cries, because he is too hot, or too cold; because he is swaddled too strait, or a Pin pricks him; because his Ordure or Excrements, make him smart; or, perhaps, he is hungry or frighted: Which of these is the Cause, may be judg'd by the Absence of all the rest; for a Child never weeps or cries without some Reason. To hinder him from weeping and crying, what he wants must be given him; and

that which gives him Pain, or Uneasiness, must be remov'd. He may likewise be pacify'd by such Things as divert him, and make him sleep, by giving him the Breast; by rocking him gently; and by singing to him. And this shews the natural Inclination Man has to Exercise and Musick.

> *The Nurse's Guide,* by an Eminent
> Physician. London, 1729.

Venetian folklore: Babies' nails should not be cut before they are a year old, or they will turn out thieves. It is unlucky to measure a baby, as it will not grow. Crying children are lucky, they will have fine eyes and broad shoulders.

> Jones, *Credulities,* 1880.

. . . let not the Nurse use any watered wine, or mixed, but mere and in his owne kynde, and let her bathe the chylde ever before she geve it sucke, after annoynting it with the oyle of *Castorium,* or the oyle of *Castum,* and let the chylde drinke every day a quantitie of this electuarie folowyng.

Take Garden Mint, Cinamome, Comin,

dry Roses, Masticke, Fenugreke, *Valerian*, Amios, *Doronicum*, *Zedoarium*, Cloves, Saunders, *Xiloaloes*, of eche a dram, of Muske halfe a dram, beate all those to powder, and confict them with clarified and depured

Honye, make thereof an electuarie, of which every day geve unto the chylde the weyght of two pence to drynke with whyte wine. If the chylde have this disease in every parte of his body, then take an ounce of Ware, and a dram of *Euforbium*, the whiche *Euforbium* ye shall beate in a morter with v or vi droppes of oyle, tyll it be perfectly beaten, then temper them together over the fire, adding thereunto so much oyle as may be sufficient to make a searecloth, and lay it to the raynes of the backe.

Thomas Raynalde, *The Birth of Mankynde*, 1565.

At three months old, it is usual to commence the use of aprons, which are made of bird's-eye diaper, or, just now, *brilliante*, a firm, close figured cambric, which will wear nearly as long. These last are bound with cambric, in solid colors, as pink, blue, buff, &c. Bird's-eye linen is usually trimmed with tatting, or any thing that wears well. At present, button-hole scollops, either plain or filled with dots, eyelets, &c., are much used; they are made in this way ornamental, as well as useful. For an infant, the 'bib apron,' round front, coming a little below the waist, with a shoulder-strap buttoning around the arm, is the most suitable. From six months to two years of age, a similar front, with back to correspond, cut of bird's-eye also. A large variety of shapes, however, are constantly to be had. The material and length is our province; no child needs an apron coming to the hem of the dress skirt, as we *have* seen them made.

The Nursery Basket, New York, 1854.

A letter to Dr Jenner:

Lincoln's-Inn Fields,
18th August, 1798.

My dear Sir,

Seven days since, I inoculated three children with cow-pox matter, and I have the mortification of finding that the infection has not taken, and I fear I shall be entirely disappointed unless you can contrive to send me some fresh matter. I think it might come in a quill in a letter, or inclosed in a bit of tin-foil, by the same conveyance, or in any other way that may be more convenient.

With much esteem, I am, dear Sir,
Your faithful servant,
Henry Cline.
Baron, *The Life of Edward Jenner, M.D.,*
1827.

Had five hundred children, from five to eight years of age; work thirteen hours, one hour and half for meals. I very soon discovered that these children, though well fed, and well clothed, and well lodged, and very great care taken of them when out of the mills, their growth and their mind were very materially injured, by being employed at these ages within the cotton-mills for eleven and a half hours per day. It is true that these children, in consequence of being well fed, well clothed, and well lodged, looked fresh to a superficial observer – healthy in their countenances; yet their limbs were very generally deformed, and their growth was stunted.

Gaskell, *The Manufacturing Population of England*, 1833.

When you have the whooping-cough, apply for a remedy to the first person you meet with riding on a piebald horse.

All the Year Round, 1873.

Children should be led to make their own investigations, and to draw their own inferences. They should be *told* as little as possible, and induced to *discover* as much as possible. Humanity has progressed solely by self-instruction; and that to achieve the best results, each mind must progress somewhat after the same fashion, is continually proved by the marked success of self-made men. Those who have been brought up under the ordinary school-drill, and have carried away with them the idea that education is practicable only in that style, will think it hopeless to make children their own teachers. If, however, they will consider that the all-important knowledge of surrounding objects which a child gets in its early years, is got without help – if they will remember that the child is self-taught in the use of its mother tongue – if they will estimate the amount of that experience of life, that out-of-school wisdom, which every boy gathers for himself – if they will mark the unusual intelligence of the uncared-for London *gamin*, as shown in whatever directions his faculties have been tasked – if further, they will think how many minds have struggled up unaided, not only through the mysteries of our irrationally-planned *curriculum*, but through hosts of other obstacles besides; they will find

45

it a not unreasonable conclusion, that if the subjects be put before him in right order and right form, any pupil of ordinary capacity will surmount his successive difficulties with but little assistance.

Herbert Spencer, *Education*, 1861.

TWO
ROYAL
AUGUST
BABIES

47

PRINCE ALBERT
(later The Prince Consort)
born August 1819.
From his journal, 21st January, 1825.

WHEN I got up this morning I was very happy: I washed myself, and then was dressed; after which I played for a little while, then the milk was brought, and afterwards dear Papa came to fetch us to breakfast. After breakfast dear Papa showed us the English horses. The little white one can trot very fast, but the chestnut one is rather clumsy. After we had seen the horses we did our lessons and then put on our boots and went to the Hofgarden. On our way home we met the little Ledermanns. Then we went home to dinner.

After dinner we drove to the Rosenau. Here dear Papa was shooting, and we went a little way with the shooting party.

Waldmann was always wanting to run and chase the partridges, but we would not let him. Sometimes, however, he ran away with the string, and we were forced to run fast after him to catch him again. We drove home, played, and then went downstairs to dinner, but that had long been over. We then visited our cousins, came upstairs again and dined, and then wrote our journals.

Now I am sleepy, I will pray and go to bed.

ELIZABETH STUART, QUEEN OF BOHEMIA
born August 1596.
Items to the amount of about 266 pounds
from the December 1601 accounts of the Lords
High Treasurers of Scotland:

For the cleithing of *Princes Elizabeth* . . . four
ellis Spanis taffatie to be hir ane goun; viii
ellis plusche to lyne the samin; iii ellis and ane
half purpour serge thairto; xvi unce and xv
drop wecht gold and silver pasmentis to hir
twa gownis; viii ell of ribbanis of colouris to
the sleiffis of hir nicht goun; iii quarteris and
ane half staming to be hir schankis; sex ellis
buckorie to lyne hir waskene bodeis and
sleiffis; iii ellis plaiding; for ane ell and ane

quarter orange craip and ane ell and ane quarter pepingo craip with tua elnis of gold and silver freinyeis thairto *to be put about hir craig.*

DISTINGUISHED
AUGUST
BABIES

NAPOLEON
born August 1769.

I had only attained my eighth year, when I already felt it painful to receive laws, even from those that have the greatest right to ordain them. I communicated this feeling to some boys of the same age as myself, but the idea was absolute Hebrew to the little brutes. My vanity was excited. What a superiority on my part! My precocity gratified me; nay, roused me almost to delirium.

Private Hours of Napoleon Bonaparte, 1816.

MARY GODOLPHIN
born August 1652.

Being demanded by the then Dutchess of Yorke for a Maid of Honour, her Mother was prevailed with to place her little Daughter att Court. This was indeed a surprizeing change of Aire, and a perilous Climate, for one soe very young as she, and scarcely yett attained to the twelvth year of her age: butt by how much more the danger soe much greater the virtue and discretion which not only preserved her steady in that giddy Station, but soe improv'd, that the example of this little Saint influenced not onely her honourable companions, butt some who were advanc'd in yeares before her, and of the most illustrious quality. What! shall I say, she like a young Apostless began to plant Religion in that barren Soyle?

Evelyn, *The Life of Mrs Godolphin*, 1847.

SIR WALTER SCOTT
born August 1771.

The chief enjoyment of my holydays was to escape with a chosen friend, who had the same taste with myself, and alternately to recite to each other such wild adventures as we were able to devise. We told, each in turn, interminable tales of knight-errantry and battles and enchantments, which were continued from one day to another as opportunity offered, without our ever thinking of bringing them to a conclusion. As we observed a strict secrecy on the subject of this intercourse, it acquired all the character of a concealed pleasure, and we used to select, for the scenes of our indulgence, long walks through the solitary and romantic environs of Arthur's Seat, Salisbury Crags, Braid Hills, and similar places in the vicinity of Edinburgh; and the recollection of those holydays still forms an *oasis* in the pilgrimage which I have to look back upon.

Autobiography of Sir Walter Scott, 1831.

GOETHE
born August 1749.

Here is a letter from his mother, quoted by Ellis.

There I sat, and there Wolfgang held me with his large black eyes; and when the fate of one of his favourites was not according to his fancy, I saw the angry veins swell in his temples, I saw him repress his tears . . . And when I made a pause for the night, promising to continue it on the morrow, I was certain that he would in the meanwhile think it out for himself; and so he often stimulated my imagination. When I turned the story according to his plan, and told him that he had found the *dénouement*, then was he all fire and flame, and one could see his little heart beating underneath his dress. His grandmother, who made a great pet of him, was the confidante of all his ideas as to how the story would turn out, and as she repeated these to me, and I turned the story according to these hints, there was a little diplomatic secrecy between us, which I never disclosed. I had the pleasure of continuing my story to the delight and astonishment of my hearers, and Wolfgang saw with glowing eyes the fulfilment of his own conceptions, and listened with enthusiastic applause.

ROBERT SOUTHEY
born August 1774.

It was a place where I was sent to be out of the way for a few hours morning and evening, for I was hardly older than Cuthbert is at this time, and though quite capable of learning the alphabet, far too young to be put to it as a task, or made to comprehend the fitness of sitting still for so long a time together on pain of the rod. Upon this occasion, when for the first time in my life I saw nothing but strange faces about me, and no one to whom I could look for kindness or protection, I gave good proof of a sense of physiognomy which never misled me yet, of honesty in speaking my opinion, and of a temerity in doing it by which my after life has often been characterised. Ma'am Powell had as forbidding a face (I well remember it) as can easily be imagined: and it was remarkable for having no eyelashes, a peculiarity which I instantly perceived. When the old woman, therefore, led me to a seat on the form, I rebelled as manfully as a boy in his third year could do, crying out, 'Take me to Pat! I don't like ye! you've got ugly eyes! take me to Pat, I say!'

born August 1785.

At a time when his additional five or six years availed nearly to make *his* age the double of mine, . . . my brother read lectures to us every night upon some branch or other of physics . . . He had been in the habit of lowering the pitch of his lectures with ostentatious condescension to the presumed level of our poor understandings. This superciliousness annoyed my sister; and accordingly, with the help of two young female visitors, and my next younger brother – in subsequent times a little middy on board a ship of H.M., and the most predestined rebel upon earth against all assumptions, small or great, of superiority – she arranged a mutiny, that had the unexpected effect of suddenly extinguishing the lectures for ever. He had happened to say, what was no unusual thing for him, that he flattered himself he had made the point under discussion tolerably clear; 'clear' he added, bowing round the half-circle of us, the audience, 'to the meanest of capacities'; and then he repeated, sonorously, 'clear to the most excruciatingly mean of capacities'. Upon which a voice, a female voice – but whose voice, in the tumult that followed I did not distinguish – retorted, 'No, you haven't; it's as dark as sin'; and then, without a moment's interval, a second voice exclaimed, 'Dark as night'; then came my younger brother's insurrectionary yell, 'Dark as midnight'; then another female voice chimed in melodiously, 'Dark as pitch'; and so the peal continued to come round like a catch, the whole being so well concerted, and the rolling fire so well sustained, that it was impossible to make head against it; whilst the abruptness of the interruption gave to it the protecting character of an oral 'round-robin', it being impossible to challenge any one in particular as the ringleader. Burke's phrase of 'the swinish multitude', applied to mobs, was then in everybody's mouth; and, accordingly, after my brother had recovered from his first astonishment at this audacious mutiny, he made us several sweeping bows, that looked very much like tentative rehearsals of a sweeping *fusillade*, and then addressed us in a very brief speech, of which we could distinguish the words *pearls* and *swinish multitude*, but uttered in a very low key, perhaps out of some lurking consideration for the two young strangers. We all laughed in chorus at this parting salute; my brother himself condescended at last to join us; but there ended the course of lectures on natural philosophy.

From his autobiography.

JAMES SILK BUCKINGHAM
born August 1786.

I was accordingly hurried off, when about seven years old, to a small village, called Hubbarton, some ten or twelve miles from Plymouth, and there placed under the care of a Mr Scott, who kept an academy for boys, of which I was the youngest among some sixty or seventy. This was a source of great misery to me, and during the year I remained here, I think I suffered more real and intense grief than during any similar period in my life. The master was a tyrant, the ushers almost worse, and the big boys tyrannised over the little ones to an insufferable degree, the example of their teachers being not only copied by them but exceeded. The food was so scantily supplied, that though in general revolting in its quality and cooking, bands of hungry boys often leagued together, to descend from their beds in the middle of the night, and rob the pantry of whatever it contained, often wrangling for the division of the spoil, but devouring it all before they resumed their sleep. The beds were hard, the clothing coarse and insufficient, and two and sometimes three boys slept together. The tasks imposed as punishments were most irksome; such as repeating from memory some of the hardest chapters in the Bible, which caused the Sacred Book to be regarded with anything but reverence.

From his autobiography.

GENERAL SIR CHARLES JAMES NAPIER
born August 1782.

His moral resolution was very early shown.
A wandering showman, a wild-looking
creature, short of stature but huge of limb,
half naked, with thick matted red hair and
beard, and a thundering voice, was displaying
his powers on the Esplanade at Castletown. A
crowd of people gathered, and, after some
minor displays, the man, balancing a ladder
on his chin, invited, or rather, with menacing
tones ordered a sweep to mount and sit on
the top, but the boy shrunk in fear from the
shouting gesticulating ogre. Charles Napier,
then six years old, was asked by his father if
he would venture? Silent for a moment he
seemed to fear, but suddenly looking up said
yes, and was borne aloft amidst the cheers of
the spectators.

The Life and Opinions of General
Sir Charles James Napier by
Lieut.-Gen. W. Napier, 1857.

JEAN PIERRE DE BERANGER
born August 1780.

It was the occasion on which prizes were distributed to the pupils; I had not the slightest claim to any myself, and I saw them conferred on younger fellow pupils without a single feeling of envy or regret. I was quite satisfied to be passed over: when – had I not what I must call the remarkable misfortune to be presented with the *croix de sagesse*; the eternal lot of college boobies? – to be candid, I had certainly some right to it, as I was neither given to play, nor insubordinate, nor noisy.

But the pupils did not fail to shout *haro sur le baudet!* This, however, did not prevent my being decorated with the cursed cross. But if any feeling of pride was conceived on this account, it was of short continuance. That very day, when the pupils of all ages who had not yet been removed by their relatives for the vacation, were assembled in the play-ground, I was standing at the railing which separated us from the street, eyeing the stalls of cakes and fruit which were stationed there to tempt the meagre

63

purses of the scholars. The small sums which relations allow to be distributed to their children under the name of *semaine,* or weekly money, were rapidly exchanged for such sweet dainties. Alas! My only pleasure was to be a witness of the enjoyment of others – for I had no *semaine.* An enormous apple, with its glowing vermillion coat, particularly excited my appetite. Child-like, I was devouring it with my eyes, when a rude voice suddenly exclaimed, close to my ear, 'Take the apple! Take it! Or I shall thrash you.' It was not the old serpent which tempted our first parents, but the terrible Grammont. His iron hand was pressing me against the railing. What feelings took possession of my innocent and candid spirit! I scarcely dared to commit the act; but terror, in conjunction with my eager appetite, triumphed so completely, that I yielded to the injunctions of my enemy; and, forgetting the respect due to my new decoration, I tremblingly put forth my hand, and seized the fatal apple. I had no sooner committed the crime than Grammont seizes me by the collar, raises the cry of

thief, and holds forth the evidence of my
guilt before the assembled school. What a
scandal! The holder of the prize for good
conduct to have been betrayed into the
commission of so heinous a fault! I was
taken into the presence of the masters; but
so great was my agitation, that I neither
heard nor understood the sentence that was
passed upon me. Doubtless, the bad
reputation of the accuser, who was detested
both by pupils and by masters, and some

kind testimonies in my favour, enlightened
the conscience of the judges.

It is certain, however, that I was obliged to
give up the cross – which Grammont, at the
first moment, had snatched from my breast.

From his own memoirs.

MARY WOLLSTONECRAFT SHELLEY
born August 1797.

The tenderness of her mother's warm heart,
her father's ripe wisdom, the rich inheritance
of intellect and genius which was her
birthright, all these seemed to promise her the
happiest of childhoods. But these bright
prospects were clouded within a few hours of
her birth by that change in her mother's
condition which, ten days later, ended in
death.

The little infant was left to the care of a
father of much theoretic wisdom but
profound practical ignorance, so confirmed in
his old bachelor ways by years and habit that,
even when love so far conquered him as to
make him quit the single state, he declined
family life, and carried on a double existence,

taking rooms a few doors from his wife's home, and combining the joys—as yet none of the cares—of matrimony with the independence, and as much as possible of the irresponsibility, of bachelorhood.

The Life and Letters of Mary Wollstonecraft Shelley by Mrs Julian Marshall, 1889.

GAMES
for the
AUGUST
BABY

A game with the five toes, each toe being touched in succession as these names are cried:
Harry Whistle, Tommy Thistle,
Harry Whible, Tommy Thible,
And little Oker-bell.

The following lines are repeated by the nurse when sliding her hand down the child's face:
My mother and your mother
    Went over the way;
Said my mother to your mother,
    It's chop-a-nose day!

This is a famous song for a young child, the nurse dancing it on her knee, and gradually increasing the ascent of the foot:
This is the way the ladies ride;
    Tri, tre, tre, tree,
    Tri, tre, tre, tree!
This is the way the ladies ride;
    Tri, tre, tre, tri-tre-tre-tree!

This is the way the gentlemen ride;
    Gallop-a-trot,
    Gallop-a-trot!
This is the way the gentlemen ride,
    Gallop-a gallop-a-trot!

This is the way the farmers ride,
    Hobbledy-hoy,
    Hobbledy-hoy!
This is the way the farmers ride,
    Hobbledy hobbledy-hoy!
        Popular Rhymes and Nursery Tales,
        collected by Halliwell, 1849.

AN
AUGUST
CHILD
IN
FICTION

AS I grew older my thoughts took a larger flight, and I frequently fell into long reveries about distant voyages and travels, and thought how fine it would be, to be able to talk about remote and barbarous countries; with what reverence and wonder people would regard me, if I had just returned from the coast of Africa or New Zealand; how dark and romantic my sunburnt cheek would look; how I would bring home with me foreign clothes of a rich fabric and princely make, and wear them up and down the streets, and how grocers' boys would turn back their heads to look at me, as I went by. For I very well remembered staring at a man myself, who was pointed out to me by my aunt one Sunday in Church, as the person who had been in Stony Arabia, and passed through strange adventures there, all of which with my own eyes I had read in the book which he wrote, an arid-looking book in a pale yellow cover.

'See what big eyes he has,' whispered my aunt, 'they got so big, because, when he was almost dead with famishing in the desert, he all at once caught sight of a date tree with the ripe fruit hanging on it.'

Upon this, I stared at him till I thought his eyes were really of an uncommon size, and stuck out from his head like those of a lobster. I am sure my own eyes must have magnified as I stared. When church was out, I wanted my aunt to take me along and follow the traveller home. But she said the constables would take us up, if we did; and so I never saw this wonderful Arabian traveller again. But he long haunted me; and several times I dreamt of him, and thought his great eyes were grown still larger and rounder; and once I had a vision of the date tree.

Herman Melville, *Redburn*, 1849.

Thus, when the anxiety was over, and he was a strong boy, full of health and activity, his will was entirely unrestrained, he had no notion of minding any of us, still less of learning. Trevor Lea could read, write, talk French, say a few Latin declensions, when Alured could not read a word of three letters, and would not try to learn.

Oh! the antics he played when I tried to teach him! Then Fulk tried, and he was tame for three days, but then came idleness, wilfulness, anger, punishment, but he laughed to scorn all that we could find in our hearts to do to him.

As to getting other help we were ashamed till he should be a little less shamefully backward. The Cradocks offered to teach him, but then, unless he was elaborately put on honour, he played truant.

He had plenty of honour, plenty of affection, but not the smallest conscience as to obedience; and Fulk would not have the other two motives worked too hard, saying the one might break, the other give way.

C. M. Yonge, *Lady Hester*, 1880.

LETTERS
from
AUGUST
CHILDREN

WRITTEN to her father, James I of England and VI of Scotland, by his daughter The Princess Elizabeth, (born 1596).

Most gratious soveraygn and dear father this gentleman Mr Haringtons returne to the court gave mee a well pleasing oportunity to present yor Ma^{ty} w^t this paper the messenger of my most humble duty to your highness thinking it I confess infinitelye long since I was so happie as to enjoy your presence wch though I dare not presume to desire, I know nothing I would so gladly obtayne And so humbly craving yor Maties blessing I will ever continue

Your Maties most obedient

daughter

Elizabeth

To the kynges most excellent Majesty
    Written by Prince Albert, afterwards The
Prince Consort, when he was six.

1825.

Dear Papa,
    We have now been a week at Ketschendorf,
and are quite well. I hope you have arrived
safe at Berlin, but come back to us soon. I
long for your return. It is very fine here. We
often stay out till near 10 o'clock, as it is
much finer in the evenings than in the day.
We were at the Rosenau a few days ago, but
unluckily the weather was not fine. The wind
was very high. We are going there again today
with dear grandmama. Pikas is with us at
Ketschendorf, but he often runs away from
us. Think of me with love.

                                    Your
                                        Albert.

RHYMES
for the
AUGUST
BABY

A UGUST brings the sheaves of corn;
Then the harvest home is borne.

Sara Coleridge (1802–1852).

A BENISON

Here a little child I stand,
Heaving up my either hand;
Cold as Paddocks though they be,
Here I lift them up to Thee,
For a benison to fall
On our meat, and on us all. Amen.

Robert Herrick (1591–1674).

LULLABY

What does little birdie say,
In her nest at peep of day?
Let me fly, says little birdie;
Mother, let me fly away.
Birdie, rest a little longer,
Till thy little wings are stronger.
So she rests a little longer,
Then she flies away.

What does little baby say,
In her bed at peep of day?
Baby says, like little birdie,
Let me rise and fly away.
Baby, sleep a little longer,
Till thy little limbs are stronger.
If she sleeps a little longer,
Baby, too, shall fly away.

Tennyson (1809–1892).

LULLABY OF AN INFANT CHIEF
(*Air*: 'Cadul gu lo.' – Sleep on till day.)

O, hush thee, my babie, thy sire was a knight,
Thy mother a lady, both lovely and bright;

The woods and the glens, from the towers
  we see,
They all are belonging, dear babie, to thee.
    O ho ro, i ri ri, cadul gu lo,
    O ho ro, i ri ri, etc.

O, fear not the bugle, though loudly it
  blows,
It calls but the warders that guard thy
  repose;
Their bows would be bended, their blades
  would be red,
Ere the step of a foeman draws near to thy
  bed.
    O ho ro, i ri ri, etc.

O, hush thee, my babie, the time soon will
  come,
When they sleep shall be broken by trumpet
  and drum;
Then hush thee, my darling, take rest while
  you may,
For strife comes with manhood, and waking
  with day.
    O ho ro, i ri ri, etc.
            Sir Walter Scott (1771–1832).

A PRAYER

Teach me, my God and King,
In all things Thee to see,
And what I do in any thing
To do it as for Thee.

George Herbert (1593–1632).

GOODNIGHT
to the
AUGUST
BABY

BEFORE dropping off to sleep perhaps you will look out of your open window at the night sky, and think of course about your baby. What do you want the newcomer to grow up to be? If you had a fairy godmother, and she could come to your bedside, what gift would you ask her to bestow? Good health of course, and happiness, but what special gift? Would you like a child of outstanding talent? Or would you like a nice ordinary child, who did not require special training and attention? Would you ask for riches, always a chancy wish, for in the fairy story riches without a qualifying virtue were inclined to go wrong? Would you ask for some gift that you yourself would have loved to have had, for instance beauty for a girl, and good looks for a boy? It is a curious thing, but few of us, if we had the chance, would accept wishes for others even if they were offered. Nobody knows what the world is going to be like in which your baby will live, nor what special attributes it will need to fit into that world, so the chances are that even if your fairy godmother could come to your bed-side, although it would be nice to have the offer, you would probably say 'No thank you, take away that wand, I'm not going to wish anything; I want my baby just the way it is.'

Noel Streatfeild